The Four Elements
FIRE

Text by Connor Dayton
Illustrations by Cecco Mariniello

WINDMILL
BOOKS

New York

Published in 2015 by Windmill Books, An Imprint of Rosen Publishing
29 East 21st Street, New York, NY 10010

Illustrations by Cecco Mariniello
Computer graphics by Roberto Simoni

Photo Credits: p. 8 offstocker/iStock/Thinkstock; p. 15 Vlada Z/Shutterstock.com;
p. 16 Rainer Albiez/Shutterstock.com; p. 19 solarseven/Shutterstock.com;
p. 21 mikeledray/Shutterstock.com; p. 26 jordache/Shutterstock.com; p. 27 Tommy
Bikales; p. 29 Alin Brotea/Shutterstock.com.

Library of Congress Cataloging-in-Publication Data

Dayton, Connor.
 Fire / by Connor Dayton.
     pages cm. — (The four elements)
 Includes index.
 ISBN 978-1-4777-9271-1 (library binding) — ISBN 978-1-4777-9272-8 (pbk.) —
ISBN 978-1-4777-9269-8 (6-pack)
 1. Fire—Juvenile literature. 2. Combustion—Juvenile literature. 3. Four elements
(Philosophy)—Juvenile literature. I. Title.
 QD516.D28 2015
 541'.361—dc23
                        2013050482

Manufactured in the United States of America

CPSIA Compliance Information: Batch # BW14WM: For Further Information contact Windmill Books, New York, New York at 1-866-478-0556
Windmill Books wishes to thank AD Books for original creation of content in this book.

Contents

The Four Elements

Long ago, the ancient Greeks believed that everything was made up of four things they called **elements**. These elements were air, water, earth, and fire. The Greeks used these elements to explain how the Earth worked.
This series takes a closer look at the science behind the four Greek elements.

Today we understand elements to be the tiny pieces that make up all matter. There are 118 elements, but fire is not one of them. Fire is a **chemical reaction**, or a change in matter.

7

Useful Fire

People have used for hundreds of thousands of years. It gives off heat to cook food or warm up a room. It also gives light so you can see in dark places or at night.

We use fire today, but not in the same ways as people from long ago. For example, we use fire to cook food, but it usually comes from a stove and not an open fire. Today, people usually use light bulbs instead of **torches** to see at night.

How to Light a Fire...

A fire needs three things to burn: **fuel**, oxygen, and heat. If you add enough heat to the fuel it breaks apart and releases gas. The gas mixes with the oxygen in the air. If the gas gets hot enough, it will make a flame.

Fuel for a fire can be many things. Wood, paper, wax, and some gases are just a few. Some ways heat can be added to fuel is by rubbing things together to make heat, banging things together to make a spark, or using a flame that is already burning.

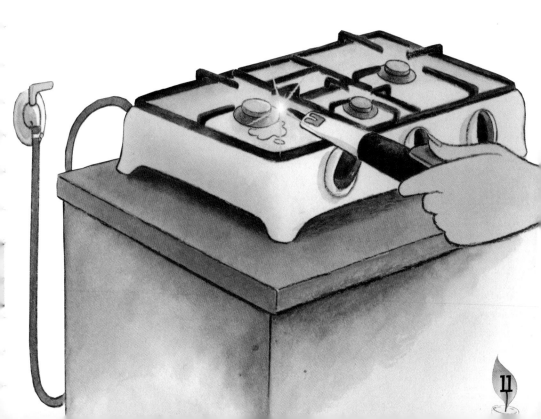

...And How to Put It Out

To put out a flame or fire, just get rid of any of the three things it needs to burn.

When you blow on birthday candles, your breath **removes** the heat. When firefighters put water on a fire, it removes the oxygen. A fire can go out if it burns up all the fuel.

13

A Huge Ball of Fire?

Fire gives off heat and light. The sun also gives off heat and light. Does that mean the sun is made of fire?

The answer is no. The sun is a big ball of gases. The way these gases **combine** is what gives off the heat and light. There is no actual fire.

15

Earthly Fires

There is something called magma inside of the Earth. It is melted rock that is very hot. Sometimes magma pushes its way out of the Earth through a volcano.

Magma is very dangerous. It will burn and **destroy** anything it touches or gets close to. It may look like fire, but it is not. Its heat can set other things on fire, though.

The Colors of Fire

One thing you may have noticed about fire is that it can be different colors. For example, the flame on a candle is usually yellow, but the flame from a gas stove is usually blue.

The color of a flame depends on how hot it burns. It also depends on what is being burned. Different types of fuel will show up as different colors when burned.

The Taming of Fire

When humans learned how to use fire hundreds of thousands of years ago, it changed everything. They were able to stay warm, cook food, light up the night, and fight off wild animals. Fire was important for survival.

Sitting Around a Campfire

Fire has been important to man since they first learned to use it. Throughout history, it has become a tradition to sit around fires while eating and talking.

People still gather around fires to cook, eat, and talk. Many people do this while on camping trips. Some people have fireplaces inside of their homes. This allows them to have a fire safely inside.

Using Fire

People use fire in many ways. For example, the fire inside a steam engine heats up water and turns it into steam. The **pressure** from the steam moves parts of the engine and moves the train.

Fire is also used to cook food in many ways. Some pizza ovens have actual fires inside of them.

Working with Fire

Many materials will melt if you heat them to the right temperature. This makes those materials easy to work into shapes. When the materials cool off, they will keep that shape.

Fire is used to melt
iron. Some artists use
fire to heat up materials to make
molten, or melted, glass. They dip
a pole into it and then shape the
glass by twisting and
blowing into the pole.

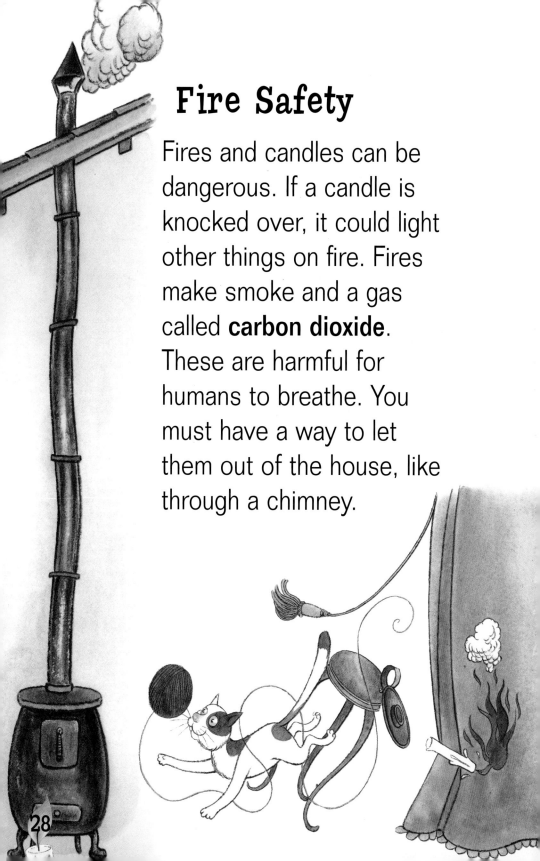

Fire Safety

Fires and candles can be dangerous. If a candle is knocked over, it could light other things on fire. Fires make smoke and a gas called **carbon dioxide**. These are harmful for humans to breathe. You must have a way to let them out of the house, like through a chimney.

Campfires are fun, but you must be careful. If a campfire is not watched, it could spread and start a forest fire. Before leaving a campfire, make sure it is completely out. It is important to always have an adult around if there is a candle or fire.

Glossary

carbon dioxide (KAHR-bun dy-OK-syd) A gas that fires make and that is harmful to breathe.

chemical reaction (KEH-mih-kul ree-AK-shun) The change that happens when matter is mixed with other matter.

combine (kum-BYN) Join together.

destroy (dih-STROY) To tear apart or ruin.

elements (EH-luh-ments) The basic matter of which all things are made.

fuel (FYOOL) Something burned to make warmth or power.

molten (MOHL-ten) Melted by heat.

pressure (PREH-shur) A force that pushes on something.

removes (ruh-MOOVZ) Gets rid of or takes away.

torches (TORCH-ez) Sticks that are set on fire to give light.

Further Reading

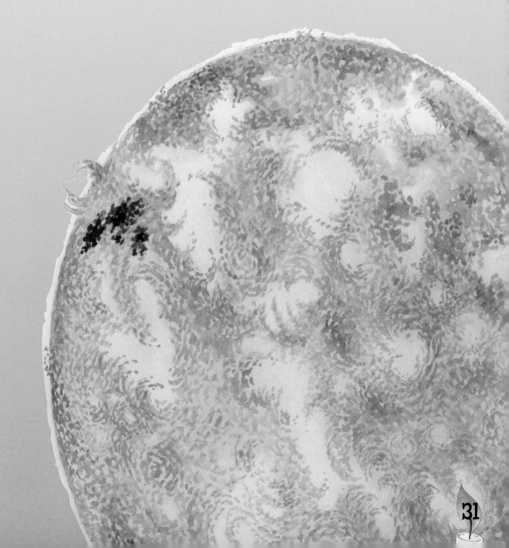

Goodkin, Celia. *Fire!: A Renewal of a Forest*. Markham, Ontario, Canada: Fitzhenry and Whiteside, 2006.

Marzollo, Jean. *I Am Fire*. New York: Scholastic, 1996.

Simon, Seymour. *Volcanoes*. New York: Harper Collins, 2011.

Index

Websites

For web resources related to the subject of this book, go to: www.windmillbooks.com/weblinks and select this book's title.

SARA HIGHTOWER